STORIES
THE ELDERS
NEVER
TOLD US

If You **Think Outside the Box,** You Should!

STORIES
THE ELDERS
NEVER
TOLD US

AIDOMOJIE OMOKHOJIE

STORIES THE ELDERS NEVER TOLD US
IF YOU THINK OUTSIDE THE BOX, YOU SHOULD!

iUniverse books may be ordered through booksellers or by contacting:

iUniverse
1663 Liberty Drive
Bloomington, IN 47403
www.iuniverse.com
1-800-Authors (1-800-288-4677)

ISBN: 978-1-5320-4878-4 (sc)
ISBN: 978-1-5320-4877-7 (e)

Library of Congress Control Number: 2018905890

Print information available on the last page.

iUniverse rev. date: 05/11/2018

To my parents and grandparents, for their immense wisdom.

To Shola Alabi, Alexander Agbo and Favour Johnson for their friendship turned brotherhood.

To all Mechanical Engineering students of Landmark University, NOBEL SET '17.

Big thanks to God for His love and grace. Heartfelt gratitude to my parents for their support, most especially my mother Mrs. Agatha Aidomojie.

I remember to acknowledge my sisters, Olubunmi, Uwa, Favour and Comfort for always listening to my morning inspirations and the final outcomes no mtter how convenient the time is.

I cannot do but say a big thank you to Jeffery Overo, and Oluwamayowa Togun for their help rendered while working on this collection; I owe you guys big time.

Thanks to all the females that inspired a lot of these poems, knowingly or unknowingly; Blessing Philips, Chidera Ejeh, Esther Obomanu, Ufuoma Deborah, Emmanuela Samuel. You all are the best.

Gratitude goes out to my roommate Kpereobong Ibanga for this time and effort put in to making this dream a reality.

Preface

Falling in love with art is something that came naturally to me as a child, "I'd draw up scribbles on my mother's freshly painted walls, on my dad's favourite book, on my sisters' take home assignments", most of which I got punished for, but of course, I got away with some, even got patted at the back by my mother at some point.

From fine arts to music and eventually poetry, I started expressing myself having in mind that art is putting what you draw inspiration from in the view of others, so as to inspire them also. I see poetry as a message and the poet as just a pointer to the situations he draws the message from.

It therefore became startling when a whole lot of my peers, people generally, run through poetry without giving it much thought, as though it were some Sudoku puzzle at the back of newspapers, but they would stare at a painting or landscape photography, or memorise long verses of rap music and get the message of the artist or derive immense satisfaction reading a prose or watching a movie.

Wondering what the challenge people had with poetry was, I stumbled upon Tolu' Akinyemi's "Funny Men Cannot Be Trusted", where he rightly put,

"these people often find it ostentatious, intimidating, boring and obscure ...... they struggle to understand or enjoy what is conventionally considered as beautiful poetry".

I saw from his book that writing poetry for people who "hated" poetry is the easiest way to make everybody love poetry.

As pointer to a message, I draw my inspiration from my Nigerian understanding of our relationships, starting from our homes and then from our general proverbs and idioms that we are well versed in, passed down to us by our elders who are always right, either in form of stories or as a form of warning or correction.

These stories our elders told us carried deep meanings but even deeper are the stories between the lines; hence the name "Stories The Elders Never Told Us". To read between the lines takes a mind that does not think conventionally but outside the box and so encourages that "if you think outside the box, you should!".

Poetry, as it were, is for people who think outside the box, who saw their everyday situation and put it in lines and verses and played it out in rhymes and rhythms, but then, it became so conventional to be referred to as "thinking outside the box".

As a way of breaking from the conventional poetry, I, without necessarily following the poetic devices structures studied in literature as a school subject, have in this collection, put out my work as a story, a message that communicates directly to those who love to read poetry and those who do not, so that this does not become like an abstract painting mounted in a gallery, understood by its painter and analysed by its viewers, but that everyone reading can relate to the stories told and feel as though the poems were written from your life's experiences.

This book, however simple to read and understand, requires "forgetting what you know" and an open mind to see how the poet views certain situation in a witty yet relatable way.

Omokhojie Aidomojie

January 2018
Benue, Nigeria.

The Thief

Every day is for the thief
including the day that he is caught
because that is the day he is awarded his title.
He is the celebrant; on the day he is caught
and we just celebrate the day that our proverbial
Mr. Nobody was finally known

Bachelor's Degree

She grew up watching the female gender taken for granted.
She belonged to the kitchen, and "the other room".
Her future was dictated once her sex was announced:
an announcement, probably a disappointment to an
　　expectant father.
She was to be sold off to a man she barely knew,
as long as he could provide her father with wine freshly
　　brewed.
Whoever really cared for her happiness anyways?
Only her mother could understand her as they parted ways.

Soon enough, she was heavy; a child on its way.
She swore she'll do everything; her child's fate to save,
were it to be a daughter, pain, she'll never get to face,
and after nine months of waiting, a girl child prevailed.
Barriers broken, Ada was sent to school
She'll read to the highest level, do what the males do
in a spite to change the female's future anyway she could.
She was to become a heroine the ladies would look up to.

She studied long and hard with on focus in mind:
with her certificate, she'll liberate every one of her kind
from physical, sexual and stereotype abuses.
She'll set up laws for rights to equal the playing field.
Her university days, today was the last.
Best graduating student, she had finally topped her class.
She was going to be *the feminist* in the long run,
only, she was handed a *bachelor's degree* after a long run.

Falling Apples

Ever heard of Humpty sitting on the wall?
Ever heard of ten green bottles standing on the wall?
Ever heard of the mighty Jericho wall?
Ever had a hacker through your firewall?

Always wondered why Isaac wouldn't just eat that apple
and why he'd rather study it instead.
After so many years, I discover, like he long ago did:
it takes something special to get anything hanging, come
    down.

I believe that everyone is special,
I believe that everyone is equal,
I believe no one could ever climb these walls I've set up.
She believed this too, so instead of climbing, she went about
    breaking.

So, after all my hold ups and hard plays,
it will surprise me to know:
I've fallen in love,
I mean, fallen hard in love.

For the Children

We sing for the children
born to fathers who couldn't raise them,
"He resembles his mother",
the words of a failed father.

You may not understand,
(unless you're Nigerian),
that a child never resembles,
his mother
unless the child is a disgrace
to his father.

We sing for the children
spoiled rotten by their mothers.
"He is only a child",
said his failed mother.

Only a Nigerian will know
that a man could still be a child
if he resembled his mother **(read stanza two again)**.

Man, and Sin

What is sin? You may ask.
Anything that is wrong! I may answer.
From a singular thought to a dreadful task,
an eyesight to an idle chatter.

Sin is not necessarily doing,
it is also not acting.
Sin is questioning God
even when He knows we're knowledgeably limited.

Sin is the very fabric that makes man,
made from the very earth the devil fell down to.
Little wonder Paul called it a corruptible body
influenced by the slightest of evil in touch.

Man has only his interest at heart,
doing good to make heaven, one of that;
man is Selfish In Nature
read the acronym, man is SIN.

Crayons

Growing up, every child wanted to be artistic.
I'd draw up scribbles on my mother's freshly painted wall,
on my dad's favourite book,
even my sisters' take-home assignment.
Whatever meant something to anyone, I left my mark there.
Conniving together, they all came up with a plan:
all the leads in pencils were to be broken after use.
That was the most frustrating time of my life,
or so I thought.

Next day in class, we were introduced to colours.
Crayons were shared round the class,
as we started scribbling, my crayon broke.

I grew up, and fell in love.
Like my pencil leads, my heart got used and broken.
I thought, "I'll never love again".

I cried so hard it drew my teacher's attention.
"What's the problem?", she asked,
"my crayon is broken", I answered, amidst the tears
She smiled back at me and said softly,
"broken crayons still colour".

Hope

The sun is hidden in fear,
gross darkness doth covers the earth.
It's like the beginning of time
in the eyes of the Uncreated and Sublime.
The clouds roar in authority,
seemingly unopposed, it claims sovereignty.
The tears of the world fall back as rain.
If only we could share in understanding its pain:
suffering and labour and penury.
This evil, unstopped, could last several centuries.
We all seek out a savior, a messiah
to deliver and save the world from this dilemma.
A sign of hope arises in togetherness,
a band of renegades, a cavalry is harnessed,
a mighty sword unsheathed beams a silver lining.
Out of the darkness, their strengths combined,
A rainbow shining.

Tomorrow Foretold

He'll leave you by the morrow.
He'll leave you there to sorrow,
because you knew not what you had,
took him for granted and played the poor lad.

He'll leave you by the morrow.
In your heart, plunged deep, a poisoned arrow
because when he needed you the most,
you despised his hurt and left him there to toast.

You'll be alone by the morrow,
begging God, a little more time to borrow
to make amends for all the past time you've lost
after you realise: he was your best, and you, his worst.

Rerin[*]

Laugh all you want now
because you don't know tomorrow.
"The last to laugh",
my mother told me,
"is not the one who laughs the best
but the one who thought of the joke
the slowest"

Change

Society is changed by the peoples' opinion,
it's the peoples' decision, somebody's discretion
to utter, to alter, to bring the solution
like salt is a solvent, you get the illusion.
Cleanse out the pollution,
purge off the corruption,
but nothing can change until something is done.
We all await the day a messiah is born
while we sleep the night till it is dawn,
"he'll be found, like Clark Kent, on a farm heaped with corn".
Our forefathers had waited for the same, but they're gone.
"Tomorrow is bright", words we force through our teeth.
It's time to stand up, be brave, carry out the proposed
fash* all who stood up to you, I mean, all who opposed
stick with your decision and, the rest you dispose
because you have to thrive with the thorns just before you
        get rose.

Funny change is a constant,
meaning change doesn't change.

**Change: the slogan of the political party that took over power
        in Nigeria in 2015, promising change for the populace but
        instead, drove the economy downwards in only two years.
Fash*: Nigerian colloquial language translated to mean put
        aside or neglect.**

Everest

The elders always cheated us.
Rude as it seems,
it is the truth I speak.
Little as I was, I was told:
"what an elder sees sitting on the ground,
You, climb the Everest, you never will find".
The older I grew,
the later I discovered:
what was to be seen,
was always on the ground.

Black

Black is not a colour, black is just a mindset.
The darkness in our hearts, placed there by TV sets
made us all limited, made us to be blinded.
It has left us bound, it has left us stranded.
I bet if our forefathers knew what we had inside us,
that the pigment of our skin could never truly define us,
he wouldn't have let the white man write a book that's about us
because, what you do not have is what you cannot give out.
Black is not a colour, black is an illusion,
black is not a colour, it's a sick delusion.
What if like that trending gown on twitter,
all blacks were really gold
and what's superficial, is the earth on us
in our impure state
but the inside, like a child's *tabula rasa*,
still pure as slate.

First Love

I died the first time I saw her.
The way she looked could tame a wild stark
the way she moved could halt a speeding car
the way she talked easily stopped my beating heart.

I had fallen for her at my first approach
as though in the woods, trying a game to poach
she was a gazelle with a swan as her coach
so, beauty and grace, she wore as a broach.

I died the first time I saw her:
ebony black skin that glistered as the stars.
My eyes first beheld the morsels on her chest
that within, held the best wines and brewed when pressed.

The beads on her waist danced graciously as she walked,
grafting a sinusoidal wave as her buttocks would rise and fall.
Her hair was her glory, well braided into one
and I died when I first saw her, because, my heart she won.

Death

Death is not as ugly as it seems,
it's only a double-faced monster.
One's death makes for both merriment and mourning
depending where you are looking from.

An enemy die, you're happy!
what of those he was friends with?
to them, death is something horrible,
to you, death is gloriously beautiful.

Death is not as ugly as it seems,
it's only a farmer with a harvest sickle
a sickle with a sharp edge that cuts and a blunt edge that doesn't
depending where you are standing at.

My Mum

For nine months, she became my apartment
and twenty-one years, I'm still her assignment.
Proving me wrong to make me better,
doing things together made it easier to get her.
My mum, she trained me
putting her pleasures behind to raise me.
Even in the middle of the night,
the words she earlier spoke would spark a light.
My mum, she's my playmate
if she's not winning, it's stalemate.
She'd be very bothered seeing me bothered,
and you'll never see her cutting corners.
Her motives are clear as crystals,
little wonder, she always glisters.
Professing my love for my mum,
is me carrying out the easiest sum.

Love

What is love anyways?
Is it the throbbing of my heart?
because that happens every day.
Is it that unstoppable smile on my face?
because I do that when I fart.
Is it the length of an embrace?
what then keeps the enemy close?
Is love only an art
of me pretending that we are not foes?
Does love happen at first sight?
and does it deepen when we're apart?
Will I ever choose love, right?

To me, love is more than a feeling
because feelings fade when we depart.
I think love is more than smiling.
To me, love is a genuine person.

Profiled

Double sided like a video tape,
the more I lean to one, the less I leave the other.
I can't trust a lot of people
as I can hardly trust myself.
I think I'm egocentric; I'm the only book on my shelf.
My caring side, I think is cripple,
that's why my crooked smile is hard to cover.
My soul is thick as grape;
so much is spilled from a little scrape,
still I tell myself that I'm never really bothered.
I'm smart and ambidextrous and knowledgeable,
but the runway feels like home and my stronghold.
Music keep me going, and the few friends that surround me:
the whinnying of my violin, than a woman's moan; more
    desirable.
The world despises me, the most honourable of my fold
because I'm queer and different, and my arrival unusually
    timely.

Cravings

My father never tasted alcohol
because his father was a drunk.
He chose to learn from his dad's mistake,
and then, he passed it down to me.

My father never carried women,
although his father was the ladies' man.
He learnt that women are a man's easy downfall,
so, he thought he should teach me the same.

I don't blame my father though,
because he was from the school of thought
That "experience was not the best teacher,
but learning from others' experience" was too.

But learning from my father made me learn nothing.
I never got to know what drunkenness felt like,
I never got to learn the pleasure of a woman,
I never got to learn to control my cravings.
Cravings, I never knew, I even had.

Project

I lie down here waiting for you to touch me
like a woman in her prime.
You promise to complete me tomorrow, but
it seems tomorrow never comes.
What you don't realise is that I'm time bound
and my day of presentation is like the coming of the Lord:
you will stand before the judges awaiting verdict;
unknown to you, I'm your chief judge.

Late

(While running late for Engr. Ibikunle's class)

I had a long night,
checked.
I woke up late sir!
checked.
The traffic was terrible,
checked.
I was involved in an accident,
checked.
I had to rush my kid to the hospital,
checked.
I tried calling in sick,
checked.

All my excuses have been exhausted,
and yet again, today, I'm still running late.

Girl with The Fancy Name

"Issabela", it read,
the little tag across her chest.
I think that's what caught my attention,
not her face, not her breasts.
Don't get me wrong,
she was as fair as the skies.
But I stared so hard,
not hearing, the menu she read out loud.

"You looked really startled at the restaurant",
that was my date complaining
"have you two met before?",
"who?", I pretended not to understand.
"Oh! Don't do that with me,
you know I caught you staring
at the girl with the *fancy* name".

Engine for a Heart

Listened to Jon's *iRobot*
and I could decipher every note
a bit quite easier than could *Shazam*
maybe because I could relate to its lyrics:

"I was a human":
when I first caught sight of you,
when I first felt something for you,
when we first started talking,
when I found myself opening up,
when I literally felt alive.

"I am a robot":
what I have come to discover,
as the make out is only a routine,
the days out, only for relief,
the *facetime*, only make-believe.
I can no longer feel the rush of blood.
In my chest, two metals clog.
I haven't been oiled in days,
I feel like I'm going for the rust,
I feel like my engine is going to knock,
and knock it will
because a heart will break from love,
but an engine will fail from rust.

The Mighty Tree

Only two sources fall a mighty tree:
the external and the internal sources.

The external source might be a mighty wind,
it might be a mighty man with a mighty axe.
Note that these external sources have to be mighty, like the tree.

The internal source might just be a tiny rot
eating daily, the inside of the mighty tree.
The tree just takes the tiny rot lightly,
until the mighty tree becomes a mighty heap.

Picture This

Now, let's picture this:
a life that's full of bliss,
free from troubles, mind at ease,
allowed to do whatsoever we all please.

Try to imagine:
a life that's without margins,
no limits at all, whether while driving or drinking,
will there be chaos or beauty within?

Let's paint a world in our minds:
where no one was ever blind,
where no one knew what it meant to cry,
where no one knew how it felt to die,
where everyone who aimed, flew high.

Just picture it, a peaceful family:
man and wife in truthful harmony,
where parents and children enjoy serenity.

The entire home starting their own world
that this present world envies and wants to be.

Straight Up

You'd rather I lied to you,
but I'd rather I stayed true,
not to the one whose heart I hold dear,
but to you, whose heart, not mine to bear.

You'd rather I beat around the bush,
try to stir you up, several buttons to push,
than simply tell you the honest truth:
my eyes want you, as *Boaz'* did *Ruth*.

You read this poem and think "what a lad!
he's too knowledgeable, and that's rather sad.
Although this his agenda clearly heads for the flop,
I must admit, I admire that he told me straight up"

Pride

Taking away my pride, takes away my everything.
Taking away my bride, takes away my choices.
Taking away my ride, takes away my freedom.

Taking away the times I cried, takes away my emotions.
Taking away my career, takes away the times I studied.
Bring back all those who died, and my childhood with them.

Taking away the truth, takes away every time I lied.
Taking away my friends, takes away every person on my side.
Taking away my family, takes away my pride.

What Reason?

One thing that has always got me confused:
why do siblings fight?
why do friends quarrel?
why do couples break up or ask for space?
To some people, answers I find bizarre;
fighting and quarreling eventually brings you closer.
To some, you should break up without becoming enemies.
You should take all the time and space you want
and then come back and act as if none of it ever did happen.

If these reasons are valid,
then I begin to wonder deep within myself:
what reason then do enemies fight?
is it for the same purpose as bringing them together?
why then do foes quarrel?
is it to make them acquaintances?
what reason can we give for civil wars?
is it so that the parties involved would re-unite,
only to act as if none of it had ever happened?

Bury the Hatchet

History never repeats itself,
all we get from it are its stories.
Series of books piled up on my shelf,
waiting to be followed up like a *Netflix* TV show.
Where are the artifacts from those great wars?
Rarely found, the swords that slew a few thousands,
hardly ever, the oars that navigated new worlds.
I've always wondered why we have
so much happenings with only books to show for it,
until I came across this saying,
idiom you might call it but it gave me a solid reason.
Our elders always did and said:
"let's bury the hatchet".

The Poet's Wail

I write about the pains I feel inside.
I try to shed this ink as tears.
I'm distressed within me.
Pen to paper; I put, and well address
my call for help to any physician
who would but care to listen.

But what do I get for a reply?

I required therapy, I got an applaud.
I desired comfort for all my unshed tears,
instead, I'm awarded a plaque.
I needed a soothing balm for my troubled heart,
in place of that, what I got was a reputation.
A reputation, I know, I truly don't deserve

My life put out there; now an entertainment.
My pigmented tears are being poured out for leisure.
My emptiness is well valued amongst those that have no
    tears to cry
and I've become a professional crier for those with tears,
    who can't
or have accepted fate, and won't cry out, like I would.

This is my blessing and this is my curse.
This wailing has become my gain and my loss.
My tears; the world has left me alone to nurse
and covered up their insensitivity by filling up my purse.
Bouquets at my feet; they toss - forgetting - my tears' source
needs patching and my heart's burns need cooling.
I desperately need to face my insecurities,

                                   because they scare me.

Dancing with My Shadows

The three of us under the light.
Identities alike but different, as it were.
I'm without a decision, as I depend on their votes,
votes of choice of what I do, of what I must become.
The next, he's the lighter of the two.
Yielding to the right, and his option also right,
but he's not persistent, doesn't coax me his way.
He's patient, quietly waiting, hoping his vote will count.
I think I'll go his way, in fact, that's where I'm headed,
but then again, the other doesn't agree.
His ways are dark, his appearance is too.
Leaning to the left and longer than the other,
he's persistent, unyielding and relentless.
Open door and effectual? He's my open adversary.
So, here I stand in this spotlight,
waltzing back and forth, like in a homecoming,
sitting on the fence.

Waiting for Love

"I'm not ready at the moment",
eager words that easily escaped her mouth,
until she found herself rolling
on the tiled Shiloh ground.

Jumoke's suitors had all gone
like a flight that could be
delayed no further.

Only then did she come
running into the airport,
ticket in hand,
patiently sitting,

waiting for love,
that had long gone

Warfare; Love Affair

"All is fair in love and war"
I always wondered what the separations was for
because love is war and we fight for love.
For a moment I thought she'd leave me
a moment longer, she thought she'll too.
In a spite to express my feeling of impending loneliness,
I held her tight, hoping to never let her go.
You could hear our hearts in syncopation beating;
this was love - my own point of view.
Then she lashed out, "why do we have to leave?"
A moment longer, she pushed out of my arms
angry she seemed, angry she sounded.
Rushing into her room, tears still welling;
this was true love - her own point of view.

Cheats

Liars always think they are being lied to,
honest people may just be too gullible.
Which is better of these two?
The liar or the one accepting to be fooled.

Liars always think they are accused of lying
so, they use another lie as proof for this established lie.
Even when he finally says the truth,
his words are like a tree without roots.

Cheats always think they are being cheated.
He'll be checking for hidden places in things not
concealed yet.
It's his nature, you can't blame him; you see.
But which is better, the cheat or the cheated?

Wanton-eyed men are never to be trusted,
once he's shifty, ensure to have him shifted,
because he'll accuse you at the slightest opportunity
of doing the very thing he'd have done if given the chance.

Learning Never Ends

Learning never ends,
we keep learning to the end.
The one who has stopped learning
is one who is already dead.

This saying is what we learnt
but truth is, even the dead, they learn.
They learn wherever they're sent,
either heaven or in hell.

You learn two things in heaven,
you learn one thing in hell.
One subject yet is mutual;
The right way to live whole on earth.

Won Over

Fall in love with her, he promised not to.
She'd said the same of him earlier
but whoever kept the records?
They were players, both in the same pitch
with unsullied reputations of never knowing love.

She was his diary, he was her dailies
so, a day never passed without their hearts touching,
although separated by a distance, which they never felt.
Soon enough, his heart became her private fiefdom.
Unknown to them both, he was hers.

The unsung untold victory unraveling,
his heart was worn out by friction.
With every touch, he shed a piece away
that isolated him from love; that made him, him.

She had won his heart, an unwanted price,
to be worn on her neck, in spite or with pride.

New Year

You know you're
in the new year
when that's all the greeting you hear,
when you enter your compound
and the fowls run away in fear.

You know you're
in the new year
when, mistakenly, the date you just wrote as today's is
a date from that of the previous year.

David and Goliath

The pen and the sword.
Two rival armies
both backed by a great number,
separated by a valley.

The pen:
Pointed at the tip,
flows with the blood of those
he spoiled in battle.
The song peddlers sing his praises,
that, "the pen is mightier than the sword"

The sword:
Edged on both sides,
the 'S' before the "word" means
silent
Unlike the pen, his chanters are quiet.
To them, "Actions speak louder than words".

Dance Off

What started as a "friendly insult"
was settled with fierce blows
one struck with a bucket
before the hands got in the dance

"We clap before we dance" †
The elders had said
what they never said to us
were the kind of dance it will be.

†   Warri proverb said in pidgin as "na from clap, na e dance
     dey start" meaning big things have little beginnings.

Book Cover

"Never judge a book
by its cover"
The old adage will tell you.
But have we ever seen
a sweet mango
with rotten skin?

Me and My Thoughts (1)

Nothing gives me more joy
than finishing a book.
Last week, I started this book,
this week, I finished with it.
Only now,
nothing gives me more distress
like finding me another book.

PART 2

"What I Long to hear is how possible it was for all our parents, no matter the schools they attended, to come first position in class – tell us these stories and we all will go to bed prepared with a longer list of the stories we want to hear".

Live

The day we are born
is the day we start to die.
We sleep and we wake
surprised about how the time flies.
The irony of it is
we do not even know we are dying
so, we go around daily
until it dawns on us
on our dying bed
remembering how we forgot to live

Stories the Elders Never Told Us

The moon is full,
Grandpa, under the mango tree
sitting on his stool
that the local carpenter, Amadi, had made for free

Like it is the full moon ritual,
today, we will hear a few stories.
Truth is, I'm tired of the usual
stories of the tortoise and mere maidens

What I long to hear
is how possible it was for all our parents,
no matter the school they attended,
to come first position in class.

Am I the only one waiting to hear
why we kneel in adoration
to pray
and stand up from a five-minute-deep sleep?

Grandpa, tell us these stories
and we all will go to bed
prepared with a longer list
of stories we want to hear.

The Girl Worth Fighting For

Yemi, a young bachelor
dressed in the colours of an ancient TV set.
You could easily tell he was a lawyer
from the way his books hugged his chest.

He has been fishing for a while now
for that lady to whom his knees would bow
in an exchange for her hand.
That's all he'll want, all in he'll demand.

Busola, she just turned twenty.
Well rounded, with an accounting degree in her bag.
Little wonder then why her suitors flooded in daily
wooing her, teasing, begging
some near, some with the corner of their eyes.

"There are so many fishes in the river"
But it was this fish every fisher wormed his hook for
This was their Argungun fishing festival
And Yemi desperately wanted this prized "**eja nla**"

eja nla: Yoruba dialect translated to mean "big fish"

Beauty and the Beast

Busola was the bride every man wanted.
"An angel to behold,
she left the norm an aroma
You should die for"

She was her colleagues envy,
the talk of the town
"She'll make a good wife"
The song on every father's lips.

Tunji, a calm, handsome young man.
He also was conversant with these eulogies
that poured constantly from his father's tongue,
in the background, his mother, giving rhythm to the tune.

"It is not every day one sees such a woman,
she may be here today, tomorrow, she'll be gone"
So, Tunji made his move, sent out banns.
The next thing we hear, Busola is his wife.

Tunji is now the envy of his mates
he had married the wife of their dreams.
If only they dreamt well.
they would see that:
Busola doesn't cook,
nor does she clean,
never will she wash
and was the first to pick a fight

If only Tunji ever dreamt,
he'd, maybe, have seen
that behind Busola's beauty
hid a ferocious beast.

Trying to Live Again

I'm awaken this morning
by the rain knocking gently on my window pane.
Its glasses are misted
just enough to make a canvas for myself.

I stand up and trace out a portrait
from my smogged reflection.
Rather quickly, the drawing bleeds out
soiling my canvas which I wipe back into glass

So is life, also
rains of hardship might knock you hard
and blur your vision
even try to change your purpose.

"Na condition make crayfish bend"
All it did was bend
not stop being a fish.
Carry your pieces, patch yourself up
And keep trying to live again.

The Elders Are Always Right

Your mother ate the last meal in the pot yesterday
you saw her, as did your sisters.
This morning, we can hear her screaming
"Who finished the meat in this soup?"

Your father is not the most patient driver.
Two days ago, he dragged his blue saloon
along a wall, leaving it a "scratch tattoo".
Today, you all are kneeling, hands in the air,
waiting for "who scratched daddy's car".

"Bisi, when you are done, come and keep the book"
Now you are not done, but you have to go
or you'd be scolded for keeping mama waiting
"Mummy, where should I drop it? Simple question it seems
"Ehn, put it on my head" is sure to be your answer.

The elders are always right
So even when they tell you to do the wrong
and the outcome is no different,
you had better not complain
or the "sorry, I was wrong" you'll get
is, "if I said, put your hand in fire, will you put it?"

Rotten Plantain, Ripe Plantain

You could hear the doors scream
as they opened silently in the middle of the night
"Funke is stealing out again,
But where she steals to, only she knows".

To think no – one knows of the habit.
First thing in the morning,
5 am was it?
There was mama Funke, re-opening for her daughter.

"She's a big girl now, she can fend for herself",
This was her mother's defense, was she ever confronted.
Her curves could speak of it, her sugar-daddies too:
Funke was indeed a "big girl".

But as the grey haired will say:
"tí ogẹdẹ bá tìn bàjẹ, ká sọ pé ọ tín pọn".
If this plantain was rottening, if were ripe,
only its eater would tell.

tí ogẹdẹ bá tìn bàjẹ, ká sọ pé ọ tín pọn: Yoruba dialect
interpreted to mean "plantain is getting spoilt, we say it
is ripening".

Good Morning

The smell of cooking smoke
welcomes itself into my room.
Normally, I hate intruders
but this one is welcome,
not because it knocks,
but because it helps announce
the presence of the neighbourhood
"mama put", akara and dodo,
frying away.

Come and Eat

Mother's eyes speak the loudest.
If it says eat, you eat
If not, your mouth should say,
"we have just eaten".

The only thing despises
his mother's eyes
are the greedy flies,
moving from plate to plate.

Israelite Journey

Wise words from the elders:
"The journey of a thousand miles
begins with a step".
What they forgot to say
is how many steps we should take.
If this detail was known,
Ralia wouldn't have gone missing
And the song never would have been sung,
"Good news is, you went a long way,
bad news is, you went the wrong way". †

† Gotten from J. Cole's rap song "Love Yourz"

The Nigerian Soiree

Pitch black night today again.
NEPA has done their part,
even the moon and stars
are significantly absent.
It's like every source of light
has joined in the on-going ASUU strike.

As we struggle to find our way
through this ~~darkness~~ Egyptian plague,
we all are too certain of these two things:
mosquitoes are preparing for
their blood meals and,
the next house "I beta pass my neighbor"
is "testing the mic" to start
its Afro Juju music.

The Town Crier

Your father is shouting
at the top of his voice.
Apparently, one of his children
has violated his instructions again.

You all grumble quietly
to yourselves using gesticulation
and eye language
"This man shouts way too much".

Your father is shouting
at the top of his voice now,
soon enough, it would be
that of one of his children.

The talking drum articulates now,
"I'm begging you now, so that
you don't beg me",
but only its beater hears what it's saying.

My Friend

Only a Nigerian will understand
when I say that the term
"My friend" is not always said
in a friendly tone or with a
friendly intention.

It is typical that "my friend"
comes just before a scolding
or immediately after a
serious "sleep inviting" beating.

Any Nigerian child would know
that you just stopped being
your father's friend when you
hear him scream "my friend",
just before the next sentence,
in your direction.

Tax Collector

You will never know that
you are a debtor until
you demand the money
you told your mother to
help you keep (hold for you).

That time, you'll come to know
that all the food you ever ate
and all the clothes you ever wore
were all eaten and worn
on credit.

You'll never know you
didn't actually "**Kọlọbi**" (syphon)
your mother's change yesterday
until she asks you
to use it to buy pepper
for next week's soup.

Red Stew

Tolu will not have
any of it this morning.
He was going and never
coming back.
He had started dating Tosin
since their first year in
the university but never
had she requested for or
given into the idea of
premarital sex.
"We are either married or
we are not".
This was their eighth year
anniversary and they were
celebrating with a fight.
Tosin was not having it
either this morning, as
she kept emphasizing
"If you can eat a food before
it is yours, you can eat
one that isn't yours".

Hide and Seek

Hidden things have a bad habit
of not knowing how to stay hidden
from the person it was intended
to stay hidden from.

"Safe places" have a bad habit
of hiding from the very person
who determined that that place
was the safest place to keep vital things.

Secrets have a secret way
of getting into the ears
of the person it was actually
intended to be a secret from.

Secrets have an open channel
of getting back to the ears
of the very person who started
the secret and yet, he is also
told to, "keep it a secret".

Domestic Violence

Only flies know the way
into a house but do
not know the way out.
The more they threaten
to leave,
the more they hit the glass
window and manage to
stay in the danger zone.

Only flies see the air
contaminated with insecticide,
and pretend not the see it
despite having a compound eye structure.
They can pretend not to see the fine
droplets in the air, but soon enough,
their breathing tracts won't be able
to deny it when they fall freely to
the ground, suffocated.

About Last Night

Which is easier to have?
An orchestra of August rain frogs
or a fighting couple as neighbours,
ready to fight about anything at all.

Two nights ago,
they fought about
whether the fan should be
switched on or not.

The night before,
it started from a friendly tease
that ended up waking the
entire neighbourhood.

~~Un~~fortunately, last night,
they did agree upon one thing:
the August rain did always
welcome little creatures that almost matched them.

Busy Doing Nothing

"Extra sheet sir", that was
Emeka crying out in the exam
hall with his pen raised in the
air a little past an hour into the paper.

Every other student, quite puzzled
that someone could call for an extra
sheet in this excruciating exam
where they could barely fill half
their booklets, paused for a second
and stared in his direction.

"Emeka, na you oh", praised Nze,
his close friend.
"No need to ask, I bet the paper
went well" concluded Nze.

"Hmm", Emeka let out a soft sigh
"I practically canceled out the
first sheet", he tried to explain.
"Only after an hour did I
realise that calculators still give you
answers when you punch in the wrong
figures".

The Unpleasant Number

Learning numbers in school is fun.
It is even said that things are as
easy as 1, 2, 3.

Numbers are not so much fun
at home, because, if you're asked
"how many times did I call you?"
or you hear your father tell you,
before I count 1 to …
and on these two occasions,
the number is 3,

the fun ends,
easy things turn hard, and,
you're in for trouble.

About Unknown Things

There is something in mummy's
soup pot that changes the smell
of the sitting room
and ushers us in from the
playing field.

There is something in daddy's horn
that dampens the atmosphere
and calls everyone inside,
telling us to comport ourselves
and read our books, or go
straight to bed.

The Intentional Blink

"Wise children always look
at their parents' eyes for
instructions, directions and
cautions", Dede would say.

As much as they always
seemed alike, we were
always able to get the
intonations of the message
and its intentions as
the blink was a language
we were well versed in.

Unfortunately, today,
with technology, the blink,
like our local languages is
going extinct.
How can I get my child to
read my eyes when his
own eyes are on his screen,
chatting away.

Noah's Ark

We all had that room in school
where everyone converged,
where everyone who wanted something,
anything, ranging from polish to
pure water to milk or cup or spoon
even for Wi-Fi, went.

Although we may deny, deep down,
we all have that one friend whom
we tend to "forget to remember" when
everything is rosy for us,
and is the first person we call when
we encounter a bump on the road.

We should all be grateful to those friends
and learn to once in a while
show up like the dove,
olive branch in our beaks,
giving something back to the ark,
in appreciation.

Half Full, Half Empty

"**Two chance**", beckoned
the shrill voice of the
conductor of a Jetta Volkswagen
with wanton eyes.

Me and my sister, who
had been waiting quite
a while, quickly jumped at
the offer ready to move.

Just then, we learnt that,
in a garage, a car of
five is always two short
of full until it is actually
full.

The Hustler

I'm awaken every morning
with a bowl of cold water
splashed on my yellow back
and across my face.

My legs are still muddy from
yesterday's work but I must
carry on today.

I start my day with a whiz
and a cough. I jerk somewhere
between the both of them but in
a while, I'm ready for the day's job
with very little in my tummy to work
with.

Soon enough, I'm packed full. Not
with food, but with my daily routine
of pickup and drop off.
Sometimes, the load becomes so much,
a rope is needed to hold them in
my bosom.

I'm hit on the head as a sign to stop
and also, to continue my assignment.
I bear my burden daily but I never give
up and I never give in.
I live to fight another day because I'm
a hustler and I fight for a better tomorrow.

I'm a Lagos **danfo**, and this is my story.

Outward Misconceptions

6:30pm and sitting in a taxi
back from my office,
reading one of the local dailies to mark time
as traffic is as bad as the front-page story.

Left of my window,
a drama scene unfolds:
A man in jean trousers and green polo shirt
is making the "yellow fever" do frog jumps.

Unknown to this unlucky "yellow fever",
the man in the green polo shirt, whom
he stopped wrongly, was an army official
driving without his uniform.

The "yellow fever" had abused his power and
was now the one being abused.
"Who now is the fool?", asked the taxi driver,
"the sleeping tiger, or the one who stepped on its tail."

The Children's Prayer

Yesterday, the skies turned black
and changed the view as to a
movie seen in black and white.

The rains were here and we could
smell in the heralding winds that
ran passed the front of our yard.

"Rain, rain, go away
come again another day
little children want to play
rain, rain, go away",
sang religiously the children
in their black pants and protruding bellies.

Today, the pregnant clouds returned
ready to break water.
The children assemble again to petition the rain.

Left to every child,
every day is play day, so
if not today, what day then,
yesterday, did they wish that
the rains will "come again"?

Employee of the Month

Tunde is back from work
tired as always,
sleeping like a sack of ~~second hand~~ okrika clothes.

He sleeps to forget those
betting slips that keep
slipping away,
slipping away with just
one match away from making
him the next millionaire.

Tunde came back from work
with slip upon slip upon slip
wishing he could just lay
his aching head down
and catch a moment sleep.

Blind Love

How could she tell that
he lied through his teeth
when he said he loved her
with his teeth looking like
a crisp starched white shirt
properly ironed?

How could she tell that
the truth was contraband to
his lips when all he ever said
was all she ever wanted to hear?

How could she tell that
all these sudden happenings
between them were too good to be true
when all these sudden happenings
were too good to be true?

How could we tell her that
this love that hit her was blind
when seeing her this happy
easily blinded our own eyes?

The elders say that "the one-eyed man
always ruled a blind kingdom".
But how do we know
who to crown king, when
the rest of us are blind?

Burnt Beans

Your aroma fills the
room like a pot of
beans, well garnished
with crayfish, palm oil
stock fish and "maggi".

We salivate your appearance,
we ready our eating utensils
and raise our anticipation
like the fire from our cooking gas,
only to meet the real you,

nothing but burnt beans.

The Believing Unbeliever

He listened to the preacher
with rapt attention,
he took note and kept on
nodding his head.

You could tell he refused
to be interrupted as he
hardly even blinked.

By tomorrow,
he will be in his office,
behind closed doors,
receiving illegal "handshakes" to open
seemingly "closed passages".

The elders only said,
"we listen with our eyes"
so we never learnt to
listen with our hearts.

Anya

I write about the eyes
as though they were the ears.

I write about the eyes
as though they were the mouth.

Indeed, they are the ears,
no doubt they are the tongue
for they hear our body language, and
they tell of our pain.

They eat our neighbours' supper
from quite some miles away
and tell all our endless stories
that keep us wide awake.

Anya: Igbo dialect interpreted to mean "eye"

The Take-off

Bayo was perpetually broke,
he knew this
as did the entire town.
What we don't know is that
he was paid fortnightly.

Where did all his money go?
On what did he spend his money?
Bayo could never really tell
nor could the entire town.

As quickly as his money came,
did it also leave his hand
as if it were spent before he even had it,
he was just a bench in the departure room

They say "money flies"
and Bayo could attest to that.
If only he could see its wings,
perhaps, he would have plucked them off

What's Cooking

Rita's suitor came today with his family
asking her hand in marriage;
a hand that had already been taken
without her family's consent.

This "knocking" process was just for formalities
as it was no news in town that she had
herself offered her hand and Peter had readily
taken it long before he came knocking for it.

Some claim you cannot have your cake and eat it
or eat your cake and have it, well not Peter;
this cake was his to eat and also to have or
have and also to eat, and he did both well.

In the backyard, you could hear her father
fuming about how **a bon marché** Rita made
herself, getting pregnant for the young chap
(who was smiling from chin to chin like a champion
successfully returned from war), to her mother who
busied herself with the kitchen' smoke.

The elders say "there is no smoke without fire".
All we could see was the smoke
what we couldn't tell was if it was a house on fire
or some rice been prepared for the guests.

Match Maker

He was the chorus to the song
that nobody forgot,
she was the credits to the movie
that nobody stayed for.

She was the reason behind
his smile,
he was the reason for all her
tears.

They say, "what God has joined
together, let no man put asunder",
but this was a jigsaw piece
that didn't even fit the puzzle.

So, we began to wonder in secret
gossips
as to who joined them together;
God, or the priest?

Empty Promises

What a task before me;
a black 50 litre jerry can,
well labelled to inform its
carrier that it is no joke.

I muster all the strength
one hand could gather and
prepare mentally as I
reach out to lift this task.

Only to meet with an
empty container readily
pulled from the ground;
those empty words of yours.

Snake

That he called you "brother"
does not mean that he loves you;
think of Abel and Cain.

That she called you "lover"
does not mean that she's got you;
think of Samson and Delilah.

That he ate from your plate
does not mean that he's satisfied;
think of Judas Iscariot.

That he said "I don't bite"
does not mean he doesn't swallow;
think "he may have no teeth".

Firewood

Body no be firewood
even firewood dey burn finish
body no be firewood
rest a little, the work no go vanish.

Body no be firewood
body no be firewood
body no be firewood
even firewood dey cool off sometimes.

PART 3

*"Mothing is more misleading like a single female
who smiles every morning to a single man in
search of a lover who is looking for him.
He is running on a treadmill and
running nowhere."*

Father Christmas

He gave anyone that asked
and he forgot to ask himself
for some.

Soon enough, he was the
one asking for a little
and he was turned away
by everyone's, "Eya, I don't
have oh".

He thought he lived by the
saying "Love your neighbor
as yourself", little did
he know that he loved
his neighbour more than
himself.

Ticking Clock

Bukky's friend wedded today
only 21 years of age.
Bukky, in her late twenties,
happy was she for her friend,
sad she was for herself.

Will her day ever come?
She begun to wonder.
She never really thought
on this before until today as
this wedding had set a timer
on her, more like a ticking
bomb.

She couldn't hear it ticking loudly
and could tell it was only
a few minutes left on it,
before it set off.

Nobody

Everybody played football in
the yard until yesterday,
nobody hit the ball too
hard,
hard enough to break
the sitting room louvres.

Everybody saw mummy's
20 naira on her bed until
nobody decided that he
needed it more than
mummy did

Everybody hates the fact
that they get punished for
the things that nobody did
and yet everybody serves
the punishment quietly
waiting for nobody to own up.

Chemistry

We felt a spark in our eyes
our hearts darted and so
we felt it was love.

Your face reddened,
my breath, a few, each moment, taken
until all that was a precipitate of what
could have been,
but quickly reacted away

effervescent little us.

Last Born Tales

Being the last child in
a Nigerian home is like
being on a playground
swing or seesaw

You love it and quickly enough,
you don't. It's your joy
and before you can
smile, it's not what
you'd bargained for.

You don't lack clothes
because everyone's smaller
one is passed down; so
also, you don't lack plates
constantly piled up in
the kitchen sink.

You never suffer while
doing your homework
and you have to be good
at dividing the meat, because,
we all will pick ours before you.

Frying Pan to Fire

You are not yet in trouble
when mummy says you should
make food for the family and
you make effort to grumble.

You just entered trouble when
the food you put on the fire
after grumbling ends up burnt
because you "purposely burnt it".

You're just waking from bed
and discover you are almost
thirty minutes late for work, so
you rush the best you can to
your office only to greet your
boss with an un-brushed mouth.

The Wordsmith

He was not the richest
he was not the smartest
he was not the tallest
nor the fairest
not the most muscular with the
broadest chest
but she stuck to him like
fleas on a stray dog
that perceive the best perfume
from what we deem stench.

Little did we know that what
he lacked in wealth and in
wisdom and in height,
he had them on his tongue
and with that, he forged the
key to her heart and the
lock too.

Curtain

Get out of the way
and let the rays of my love
hit her straight in the face
and wake her from her
seemingly drowsiness.

Don't stand any longer between us
you misguiding piece of cloth
and let her see me for who I really am
while I am here, because,
patient as I am, I will not woo forever.

You can come back up when
the moon comes out and help me
shield her from his enticing light
as he is an unfaithful lover,
gone just as you fall in love with him.

Village Goat

He chews and chews
and chews and chews
and chews and chews;
not in a hurry, not
readily distracted.

He swallows it for a
second, or so we think,
and just when we think
his grumbling has ended,
John brings the issue back
again.

So he chews and chews
And chews over and again.
Poor four bellied animal.

The Cross Road

She'd wait every day at the way
junction she knew he'd pass to
and from work so he'll but
notice her.

Were she not told by her mother
that ladies don't chase men,
she'd have caught him long ago
for she was a good runner and
apparently, he wasn't.

He on the other hand,
every morning, knees on the ground,
head bowed, asking for his daily
bread and a wife to bake the bread.

"We played the flute for you, †
and you did not dance;
we sang to you a dirge,
and you did not cry."

†   Coined from the Bible's Luke 7:32 explaining a set of
confused people who do not know what they want even
when it is handed to them on gold platter

Me and My Thoughts (2)

I don't like my mobile phone
for anything; not for calls,
not for chit-chats, not
social media, nothing!

The only thing I like my
mobile phone for is that
distinctive chime I'm so
familiar with.

I know it in my sleep
I know it when I eat,
I smile and know it has to be,
the sound of a credit alert.

My Ex-Girlfriend

We used to love playing chef
in our kitchen's backyard,
sand stuffed in our mouths,
enjoying our special meal
with secret recipe.

Whatever removed that special
spice from our backyard sand?
Whatever made us grow and
lose taste for it?

The spice we stuffed our
mouths with happily, now
spoils our mood when we
crunch it in our oil beans
or fried groundnuts.

Are We There Yet?

"Who asks questions does not
miss road" until
you ask a man, whose wife
is in labour, directions to
the nearby village and
you drive confidently to
a maternity home, two
hours later.

Nothing is more misleading
like a single female who
smiles every morning to a
single man in search of
a lover who is not looking
for him. He is running on
a treadmill and
running nowhere.

Choice

"What do you want?"
She asked him like he had a choice
"What do you think I want?"
He asked her like she could read minds
if only he had a choice
maybe he'd not have chosen her
if only she could read minds
maybe she'd have known that actually
he had no alternative for her.

First Time

Mummy always complained of missing soup meat
which nobody seemed to know the whereabouts of.
Daddy always punished us for missing money
that we felt he had leaking pockets.

Adamu always looked fresher than the rest of us
that only ate one piece of soup meat but we
felt he had better genes than the rest of us.
He always had spare cash than the rest of us
but we felt he had better savings methods than the
rest of us.

Today, Adamu was caught red handed
meat in his mouth, hands well-oiled like it
took a scuba dive into the freshly made soup.

Well it was his "first time", so we couldn't
really blame him for the previous missing soup meats
nor could we accuse him of daddy's missing money.

Real Face

We put our lives out there
frame by frame, upload by upload
hoping to find our perfect partner that's'
telling her own story that particularly
suits our expectations.

We put our hearts out there
not thinking of the risk that
when you finally meet your
social media girlfriend,
the girl in the picture may
not actually look like the
girl in the picture.

Woman Wrapper

Whose concern was it that Jide
would spend whenever Jane would
stand and sit when she'd sit
or find a reason to go out would
she wants to use the rest room?

What did he care that his male
folk laughed secretly behind him
the way he followed his lover
from pillar to post like flies to a
bottle of a hard liquor.

Well it was no one's concern
and he cared for nothing him
being called "woman wrapper",
in fact he prided in the fact that
he was, as he knew just how
much yard of it he was.

To My Jungle Boots

What relationship is tighter
From the way I love you to my feet?
You may not necessarily look charming
But for our situation, you fit,
Fit so perfectly, it's like the rhythm in our beat,
A beat we make effortlessly, marching under this heat.

The march is slow
But still we go;
Yet you carry on, soldiering away with grace.
You would make it through and through
And I will carry on too because I'm encouraged by you.

Goosebumps

Don't just give me the chills
that begin within and show
on my skin, rough enough
to tell the world I feel a
little something or something
way more than a little some
thing for you.

Don't just make me feel like
this feeling is here to stay
and abide with me if all
I am to you is a fragile
skin and you, air felt
goosebumps.

Me and My Thoughts (3)

Aren't you just look beautiful?
Aren't I just a beauty's fool?
Dark as cola and shaped as its bottle too
tasty as its content, radiant as the full moon.
I'm glad I have a sweet tooth.

They say sweet things kill
but I'd rather die smiling than
live on bitter thoughts of how I did not
let your love kill me.

Kill me my dark soft lover
kill me cube by cube
kill me sip by sip
let's see who finishes who first.

The Wait

Sitting patiently waiting for
this time to move and
welcome the next week;
but watching the second hand
tick is as exciting and watching
freshly painted walls dry

The room is hot and I, as meat,
can feel my tolerance break down
while reaching the climax
another hunger

This hunger may never be filled;
not until this wait is finally
over, so like the biblical burning
bush, let's feed this hunger but
never grow fat.

Bitter Afternoon

Sitting under a mango tree
calling out to the pretty lady
hawking oranges under the hot sun
hoping to quench this thirst with as
much of her products
my little money can acquire.

Unfortunately, the only product
my currency can purchase is
the pretty smile soon turned
into a bitter hiss that resounds
from those well-rounded lips.

I blame you, this stupid mango tree!
Why can't you bear ripe fruits all
year round and avoid me this
embarrassment?
I will sit here, for as long as it is
required, eagerly awaiting your
ripening.

About You

You really think you matter
to me, don't you?
You really think that part
of my world revolves around
you, don't you?

Don't you just sit down and
smile to yourself thinking, that
I might just be thinking about
you?
don't you anticipate my messages
hoping it may just be a new
poem written for you?

Yes, my dearest lover,
you do matter to me
and maybe my world revolves
around you.
You would be right to smile to
yourself because I'm thinking about you
and most definitely, my next
message to you is a poem written about you.

Boundary

Follow those footsteps
follow those swaying hips
follow those well braided hair locks
follow that properly made up face.

Follow your heart
until you hear the sound
of a dane gun or
freshly sharpened cutlass scrapping the ground
calling for your head
for daring to follow
your heart's desire

to her father's house
without kola or palm wine
brought in by your kinsmen.

Who is Aidomojie Omokhojie?

Aidomojie Omokhojie hails from Edo State, Nigeria. He is the only son of his parents, Mr. and Mrs. Aidomojie and has four siblings, Bunmi, Uwa, Favour and Comfort.

He bagged a bachelor's degree in Mechanical Engineering from Landmark University, Omu-aran, Kwara State and is a Graduate Member of the Nigerian Society of Engineers.

Stories the Elders Never Told Us is his first poetry collection and is one he hopes reaches out to everyone who "thinks outside the box".

Omokhojie is currently a corps member serving in Makurdi, the capital city of Benue State, Nigeria and can be found on Instagram and twitter (@cr7chuks)